This book changed my life! It helped me to grow in self-awareness as a leader, recognizing not only my own strengths, but also the strengths of my team during a challenging season. Coach Pete's sharing of real-life stories, practical tips, and clear action steps gave me the strategies that I needed to both grow my team and have the confidence and courage to make a significant career shift.

- Alia Eyres, former CEO of Mother's Choice, and Founder of Typhoon Properties

I devoured the entire book in one sitting and then went back to Chapter One to begin the real work on myself. As a leader, I can't wait to share these tools with my team to take our successful program to even greater heights.

- Rachel Thomas, Senior Director, Transplant Institute, Memorial Healthcare System

A book to return to again and again. The simple yet concise chapters are a North Star to get back on track.

- Adam Norse, Global Talent Consultant

Over the years co-hosting the *Transform Your Life* podcast with Pete, I have seen him constantly deliver incredible insights and practical tools. *Align with Your Design* brings together transformative wisdom based on Pete's experiences as a top-level executive coach.

- Steve Chua, Executive Director of Steve Chua International Coaching, President and Co-Founder of From The Insight Out, LLC

To the professional about to begin this book, it is without hyperbole that I tell you the concepts presented here by Coach Pete have profoundly transformed both my career and my life.

- Michael Pompey, Chief Information and Transformation Officer, Girl Scouts of Eastern Pennsylvania

This book's "no fluff" approach unfolds clear, attainable steps toward obtaining a meaningful career. The results are proven... first in Coach Pete's own life, and then in others.

- John C., Manager of Technical Specifications

This book is perfect for mid-career professionals seeking clarity and purpose in their lives.

- Peter Bonanno, Continuous Improvement Project Manager

If you're looking for a concise and practical book to guide you through a process of clarity about your design, then you've found the right one. Coach Pete skillfully guides you through the process of revealing your true design and then taking a leap of faith to realize it.

- Samantha Stokes-Baydur, Chief People and Culture Officer, Open Society Foundations

Concise yet profound.

- Nané Pr'Out, Director of Information Technology

I particularly enjoyed the process Pete described in the Ask Your Heart section, and the clarification between desire and object of desire. Light bulb moment for me!

- Dale Young, ACC

The content of this book will change your life. It did mine. Coaching transformed my mindset: from trying to overcome my weaknesses to exploring and exploiting my strengths for maximal impact.

- Wes Anderson, Founder, Clarion Solutions Group

If you do the work, follow this program, and take it seriously, you will find your true self. It's not easy to dig down deep into who you are, but if you follow the steps, you may be amazed at what you've been missing in your life.

- Vince C., Owner, Modern Home Contractors

Align With Your Design gave me valuable insights on aligning my strengths and purpose with my work life. It's a helpful resource for anyone feeling stuck or seeking to make meaningful changes in their career.

- Ryan Crittenden, Ph.D

Coach Pete questions the conventional advice that we can do whatever we set our mind to. Instead, Pete will lead you through a proven process to discern how you've been designed and how to best leverage that design.

- Andrew Lincoln, Finance Director

A must-read for anyone seeking fulfillment in both life and work.

- Chris Boué, Director, BHS Connect

ALIGN WITH YOUR DESIGN

7 Steps to Find Clarity and Transform Your Career

By Pete Cafarchio, PCC

Align with Your Design

7 Steps to Find Clarity and Transform Your Career

Copyright © Pete Cafarchio (2024)

DEDICATION

This book is dedicated to my many clients who constantly inspire me with their willingness to challenge themselves and courageously lead others. I learn just as much from you as you do from me. It's a true honor to serve you.

And to my wife and best friend, Lynn, who has patiently walked with me on every step of this amazing life journey.

ACKNOWLEDGEMENTS

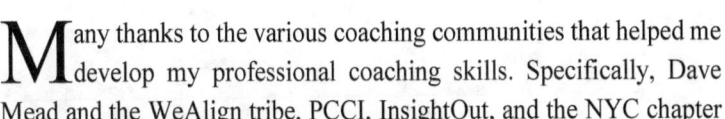

Many thanks to the various coaching communities that helped me develop my professional coaching skills. Specifically, Dave Mead and the WeAlign tribe, PCCI, InsightOut, and the NYC chapter of the International Coaching Federation.

I'm deeply indebted to my clients. They are the ones who put in the hard work of transformation, and give real-life proof that these principles work when they're applied. I salute all of you and will never stop cheering you on.

Thanks to Carlene Hill Byron, the editor on this project who kept me moving forward and gave me space for my "verbal processing."

My brother from another mother, Greg Wallace, thanks for believing in me and reminding me that I'm a "leader of leaders" each week when we get together.

Steve Chua, you're a great collaborator, podcast partner, and friend. You contributed to making this book a reality in ways you don't see.

Thanks to Transform Our World and Ed Silvoso for all the positive affirmations and for giving me opportunities to share these principles with our global tribe.

Most of all, thanks to YHWH, the author of all wisdom and the giver of life. I don't deserve all your goodness toward me, but I gladly receive it.

PREFACE

I have read a number of books whose stated purpose is to help me become a better version of myself. But to get to that better version, the authors of most of those books asked me to do what they did. Such authors think that if I mimic them, I will be successful too. But I don't want to be a successful *them*; I want to be a successful *me*.

So, *how utterly refreshing* to encounter *Align With Your Design*, a book that guides me into an examination of my self—my self-awareness, self-acceptance, and self-improvement. As Coach Pete recognizes, each of us has a unique pattern of talents, experiences, and motivations that make up who we are. His approach to building our confidence is to leverage *his* strengths to engage us in a process that leverages *our* strengths. (That's his superpower.)

If we're honest with ourselves, one of the reasons we buy someone else's self-help book is that we don't have the skills and confidence to build on those things that make us unique. Our tendency to second-guess ourselves creates paralysis by self-analysis. And to ponder our life purpose can cause us to spend an inordinate amount of time thinking about ourselves.

As Pete Cafarchio points out, self-reflection is not an exercise in selfishness. At the end of this process, we will be able to focus our energies outward on our relationships, our work, and even our play with renewed energy and increased confidence.

And how utterly amazing!! A self-help book author who trusts us to help ourselves. In *Align With Your Design,* we, not Coach Pete, are accountable for the results. In my years of experiencing Coach Pete's work one-on-one, and in small and large group settings, taking accountability is one of the certainties. It's not unusual for me to be on a personal call with my friend, Pete, sharing what I plan to do to improve a situation or to make a lifestyle change and hear him ask, "So, when are you going to do that?"

To be sure, Coach Pete is an exceptional guide, but he has placed us in the driver's seat. In our hundreds of conversations, I have rarely heard, "This is what I would do."

Thus, it's no surprise that the contents of each of the chapters in **Part 2: The Align Your Design Framework**—emphasizes our role as the active participant in our journey. We are introduced to a principle, we are given an opportunity to see the principle in action (no abstract theory here!), we are asked to apply the principle, and then we are directed to take action.

Because accountability is one of the certainties, Coach Pete writes, "Don't just read through them; do the exercises in each chapter and capture the results." As you do so, don't be surprised to hear a voice ask, "So, when are you going to do that?"

And how utterly useful!! A self-help process that is transformational. For all of the focus on ourselves, the benefits of completing the Align Your Design framework extend far beyond feeling more confident about ourselves.

The contents of **Part 3: What's Next**, help us transform all areas of our lives, including our family, our community, and even our play. But crucially, Coach Pete helps us leverage our newfound strengths in our work life. In this instance, our focus on self is not about us; it's about the increased value we bring to our work environment.

And finally, *how utterly enjoyable!!* This is a self-help book that is not drudgery to read. Coach Pete's use of analogies, anecdotes, and illustrations (Viola Davis lacking in confidence? Who knew?) contributes to a great read.

Enjoy!

Greg Wallace, MA, JD, D.Min.

President, The Wallace Group

TABLE OF CONTENTS

Dedication vii

Acknowledgements..ix

Preface xi

PART 1 There Has to be a Better Way 1

Chapter 1: Is This All There Is?...3

Stuck, Stuck, and More Stuck 5

What About You?...6

Imagine a Better Future...7

Chapter 2: Introducing the Align Your Design Framework 9

Align Your Design Overview...9

How to Use the Align Your Design Framework 12

Chapter 3: Helpful Mindsets..15

PART 2 The Align Your Design Framework 17

Chapter 4: Ask Your People: Others Can See You Better Than You See Yourself 19

The Principle 19

See It In Action...20

Apply It 21

Ask Your People: Summary..24

Chapter 5: Ask an Assessment: Tools Reveal How You're Wired 25

The Principle 25

See It in Action...26

Apply It 27

Ask An Assessment: Summary 30

Chapter 6: Ask Your Setbacks: Your Tests Become Your Testimony....31

The Principle 31

See It In Action..33

Apply It 34

Ask Your Setbacks: Summary 35

Chapter 7: Ask Your Heart: Your Passions Fuel Your Actions 37

The Principle 37

See It in Action..39

Apply It 41

Ask Your Heart: Summary...43

Chapter 8: Ask Your History: Your Past Holds Powerful Keys to Your Future..45

The Principle 46

See It In Action..46

Apply It 47

Ask Your History: Summary...51

Chapter 9: Ask Your Creator: You Were Designed for a Purpose 53

The Principle 54

See It in Action..55

Apply It 58

Ask Your Creator: Summary...62

Chapter 10: Ask a Professional: A Trained Guide Can Accelerate the Process 63

The Principle 63

See It In Action..64

Apply It 65

Ask a Professional: Summary 67

Chapter 11: Bringing It All Together 69

Some Thoughts on Finding Clarity 69

Summarizing Your Work 70

PART 3 What's Next?..75

Chapter 12: Aligning Your Work 77

Jason Found Clarity 79

Renee Found Clarity 80

Chapter 13: Take Action! 83

Get to Work on What You've Discovered 83

Action Brings Clarity 83

Set, Own, and Update Your Goals 85

The Most Important Key 86

Chapter 14: How I Aligned with My Design............................. 87

Conclusion 91

An Offer 91

Summary of the Key Principles in This Book 92

About Coach Pete 95

Top Recommendations for Further Reading 97

About the Transformation Stories You Just Read 99

PART 1
THERE HAS TO BE A BETTER WAY

CHAPTER 1
IS THIS ALL THERE IS?

Michael is a client of mine who, by all appearances, looked successful, but he was frustrated and bored. When he came to me for coaching, I could see that he was a very bright, hardworking guy. A man in his early fifties, he worked as the head of technology for a group at a big city government agency. There, he had pioneered a very effective program to empower at-risk youth. The program was so successful that other major US cities asked him to help them replicate it in their communities as well.

After a couple of years, political appointees and bureaucrats took over and made a series of bad decisions in his department. The new, small-minded management didn't appreciate Michael's ideas and vision; they just used him to keep the program in maintenance mode while they took credit for the results. With no advancement or growth, Michael found himself bored, languishing, and underpaid. He was over-talented and working under clueless leaders. He just wanted to get out of there.

> *Go where you're celebrated, not where you're tolerated.*

What Michael didn't realize—and what many professionals struggle with—is that it's possible to realign their careers with their core strengths if they can just get clarity first. So when Michael hired me as a coach, we engaged in the Align Your Design framework—the same one I'm going to take you through in this book.

Along the way Michael rediscovered his exceptional talents, all of which were strongly validated when he asked friends and family what qualities they saw in him. It was like his eyes were being opened to his potential once again. He also recognized how the big wins across his career arc dovetailed with his personality assessment results. That, in turn, helped him clearly articulate his business value. Then, with newfound confidence, he started applying to job openings.

Michael found a new role with more pay, running the entire IT department in a larger organization. He found his voice. He discovered that he's actually an exceptional leader in many regards. In fact, the other senior department directors at his new organization willingly follow his leadership direction in other areas outside of his IT expertise.

As you can imagine, such a positive turnaround at work gave him momentum for his personal and home life as well. He was able to focus on his marriage, health, and hobbies with renewed energy.

Michael took action that transformed his life. And you can, too.

Picture what it would feel like to stop having to prove yourself to people who don't appreciate you. Imagine no longer trying to be someone you're not or constantly comparing yourself to your peers. How would it improve your confidence if, like Michael, you had real clarity on what you do best and what to avoid, and could make smart choices to stay in your zone of effectiveness?

This is the kind of clarity I help my clients obtain. I'm Coach Pete and it's my honor and privilege to serve people—some just like you—to help them rediscover their inner greatness, get unstuck, and move forward with a renewed sense of purpose.

As a Professional Certified Coach (PCC), I've helped more than 300 clients transform their lives and crush their goals. I absolutely love what I do because every day, I get to see the power that insightful encouragement can have in people's lives. (You can read more about how I got here in Chapter 14.)

Countless adults have given up on the idea that things could improve. They often come to me for a career change, mid-life transition, or because they are just deeply dissatisfied with how their lives are playing out. The upward trajectory in their earlier years seems to have stalled, and they now ask themselves, "Is this all there is?"

Stuck, Stuck, and More Stuck

You might identify with one of these clients and their stories.

Passed Over and Turning Cynical

Jason is a married man in his mid-forties who excels at what he does. When we met, he worked as a senior product manager for a software company that serves the financial services industry. He has a great work ethic, is smart, and at the time he really wanted to become the company's Chief Information Officer. It seemed like the logical aspiration in his career. CIO is the top technology leadership position in many companies, and it had been his ambition since the day he entered the field decades ago.

Jason's subordinates loved him because he helped develop their skills, gave them increasing levels of responsibility, and served as a coach, not a boss. Jason's superiors had nothing but good things to say about his leadership and results, but they also weren't helping advance his career. Realistically, Jason knew there were fewer opportunities for advancement because the more senior people were choosing not to retire, holding onto the top positions. And his peers posed stiff competition for the few spots that did become open.

Jason thought he could "power through" his sense of professional stagnation, but the longer it continued, the more he found his motivation waning. He felt passed over, not good enough, and couldn't see the way forward. And with his confidence eroded, he wasn't motivated to look for a job at a new company. His family and friends noticed that he'd lost his overall optimism for life and had grown more cynical.

This is not what he set out to do in his early twenties. And he was losing hope for the second half of his career.

A Go-Getter Who Is Still Waiting

Renee is in her late thirties and she's a real go-getter with a great work ethic and loads of talent. When I began coaching her, she was working as a tenant liaison for a huge commercial real estate management company. She knew how to get results and her clients loved her, as did most of her co-workers.

She's done "all the right things" in terms of schooling and work and was promoted early on, but now she can't seem to get ahead. She is very responsible, and she finds it hard to say no to the extra duties the company asks her to take on. She's working very long hours and taking on extra work to make a good impression, hoping for a promotion. But all that happens is she gets even more work heaped on her.

Now, she's feeling used as she sees less diligent peers get the promotions she wants. But she's afraid to push back, fearing it will harm her reputation and her advancement. To make it even worse, she reports to a toxic senior leader who has a history of causing her direct reports to quit just to get out from under her negative influence.

In short, she's been waiting for her company to reward her hard work, but she's losing hope that it will ever happen. And, like Jason, she is also too exhausted to look for another job.

What About You?

Are you feeling stuck like Michael, Jason, and Renee were? Do you dread going to work on Monday? Are you overworking as you try to prove yourself but find that your career is stalled anyway? Do you feel isolated and alone at work? Are you carrying that feeling into the rest of your life, distancing yourself from the very people who would encourage and support you?

If so, you're not alone. But the good news is that these people were able to change their situations for the better. I'll tell you the rest of Jason and Renee's stories later in this book. But for right now, I just want you to know that the framework that helped them is the same one you'll discover in this book.

Here's the thing: people who feel stuck often have handed their validation over to someone else, typically their employer. Like kids waiting to be chosen for a playground team, their inward cry is, "Pick me! Pick me!" But just like the cool kids who ignore potential teammates, the employer may not be concerned about what benefits you. After all, their primary obligation is to hit organizational objectives and to satisfy stakeholders.

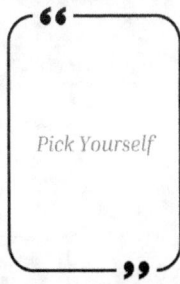

Pick Yourself

To reverse this, you need to take back control of your identity and become *internally validated*. In short, you need to pick yourself.

And no one else can or will do this for you. You alone must own the responsibility for it and take action. This book will show you how to do that.

Imagine a Better Future

Here's what you can look forward to if you apply the framework that I'll describe in Part 2:

- You'll have a clearer sense of your life's purpose.
- You'll determine the type of work that uses the talents and skills that energize, rather than drain you.

- You will have redeemed the big mistakes you've made in your past and leveraged them to make a positive difference in the world.
- You'll conquer self-doubt and low self-esteem and boost your confidence.
- You will have identified the clear, concise language that quickly lets people know the value that you bring and how you can help solve their problems.

If this sounds like what you're looking for, then dive into the next chapter with me to start your journey.

CHAPTER 2
INTRODUCING THE ALIGN YOUR DESIGN FRAMEWORK

For years, I personally struggled to understand my own place in the world. I worked in many different fields (civil engineering, technology start-ups, food service, non-profit fundraising, group facilitation, human services, etc.). Over time, through trial and error, I eventually got the clarity I was looking for. A quick note in my defense—I don't want you to think that I was failing in these roles. In fact, I did quite well (top salesperson, designed and completed a successful capital campaign, public speaking accolades, trained a global network of coaches, helped grow and sell a tech company for $40 million). Still, I was just hungry to try new experiences and keep challenging myself. Some people have described me as a "renaissance man."

Through my many experiences, I found tools and nuggets of wisdom that were super helpful. I've systematically tested these tools with scores of my own coaching clients, and I've selected the very best ones. Now I'm passing them along to you in a simplified format to streamline your own discovery process. You can be confident that these aren't simply academic theories. This approach gets results.

Align Your Design Overview

The Align Your Design framework is structured to help you view your life purpose from seven different perspectives. Those include:

1. Other people's observations

2. Scientific assessment tools
3. Challenges you've overcome
4. Passions that drive your life
5. Your history of accomplishments
6. Impressions from your spiritual life
7. Insights from speaking with a professional

Part 2 of this book devotes a separate chapter to each perspective, along with explanations of the underlying principles and practical exercises for you to complete.

You'll capture your insights along the way and then bring it all together in a summary.

Why "Align"?

I selected the word "align" for a very specific reason. There's a popular concept in the field of personal development that goes something like, "You can become anything you want to be." While on the surface that sounds motivating, it ignores the limits every person faces due to talent, genetics, upbringing, culture, lack of opportunities, and a host of other factors. No, I can't become an Olympic swimmer. No matter how much I practice, I can't change my physiology (short arms, short legs, and a dense torso). I also wouldn't make a very good accountant. Repetitious details drive me crazy—I'm wired to think outside the box and create new things.

A much more effective path to success is to recognize the strengths you *do* have and then make choices that leverage those in your vocation and personal life.

You might ask, "But Pete, isn't there a role for self-improvement?" Of course there is, but self-awareness is the starting point. Only then can you make smart choices about which strengths you should develop and which weaknesses you need to mitigate so they don't hinder your

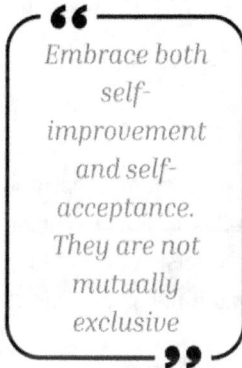

Embrace both self-improvement and self-acceptance. They are not mutually exclusive

performance. A balanced approach is to embrace both self-improvement and self-acceptance. They are not mutually exclusive.

Why "Design"?

Each of us has a unique pattern of values, talents, experiences, genetics, and motivations that help to make up who we are.

You might believe in a divine Creator who designed you with love and intention. Or you might believe in some form of evolution. You may even land somewhere in between.

But no matter your frame of reference, I think we can all agree that your identity is unique—no one else on earth has your exact genetic combination. Starting from that understanding, the Align Your Design framework will help you clarify and articulate your uniqueness. I've used it with clients who hold widely varying worldviews, and they all get good results. You will, too.

Nature or Nurture?

There's a long-standing question in the field of personality theory: Are we solely a product of our genetics (nature) or of our experiences and upbringing (nurture)? It's a good question to ponder. Why do siblings raised in the same household wind up so very different as adults?

The short answer is that both nature and nurture contribute to who you are today, and the exercises in this framework draw from both sources.

Some of my more curious clients will sometimes question the accuracy of the methods I'm going to present and try to analyze whether their results are fixed (nature) or subjective (nurture). My simple advice is not to go there. Instead, just take the results at face value. No matter the source, you are who you are today.

How to Use the Align Your Design Framework

While it's helpful to work through the exercises in order, that approach is not required to get their full value. Instead, think of it and yourself like a multi-faceted diamond. It takes all the facets, reflecting and refracting light in their own ways, to make a beautiful, comprehensive gem.

You can choose to do the exercises from chapters 4–10 in any order you want; however, I suggest doing Chapter 9 after you've done the others since it can leverage your insights from all the previous chapters.

And keep in mind that this is a general framework, not a formula that will give you an exact answer. Make it your aim to get *better* clarity, not *absolute* clarity.

Go Slow and Capture the Insights

The exercises are designed to evoke deeper reflection into your life. To that end, you won't want to rush through them. One suggested cadence is to do one chapter per week. That way you'll have time to fully engage with each perspective and consider its implications.

The answers you get from some of these exercises will be illuminating—that's great! I love when I get an epiphany.

Some of the answers might be obvious. Good for you. That means you already have good self-awareness.

And one or two exercises might not yield anything for you right away. That's okay too. Just take your time and work through the exercise at your own pace.

Trust the Process

But no matter what, trust the process. Don't just read through the book; do the exercises in each chapter and capture the results.

Here are some more practical tips that others have found helpful:

- Keep it organized. At the end of each chapter, you'll be asked to capture the top insights you gained from the questions and exercises. Log your answers in a journal, an electronic file, or whatever works for you.
- Each chapter contains a summary of the key points and a prompt to highlight the insights that you found most valuable.
- Consider doing this with a friend. You can keep each other accountable and share insights along the way.
- Find a quiet, uninterrupted place and time to be alone while working on these exercises. You can listen to mood music and surround yourself with favorite things, but don't allow yourself any distractions.
- Try not to overthink or overcomplicate things. Often, your gut is telling you the right things. Trust it.
- If you get stuck on an exercise, just skip it and go on to another chapter. You can always come back to it later.
- When ideas occur to you unexpectedly later in the day, find a way to capture them, even if they're not fully thought through. Use whatever is handy to make a note that you can reference later. I like, for instance, using the voice-to-text function on my smartphone.
- If you get an "Aha!" moment that leads you down a rabbit trail, just go with it. Stay in the flow of thoughts and capture them.
- Some of these exercises might take a few days to complete. For instance, when you ask your friends and family for their feedback in Ask Your People, you could go on to another chapter while you're waiting for their responses.

Sometimes, our own thought processes can sabotage our progress. In the next chapter, I'll address some mindsets I see when coaching my clients and how to overcome each one so you don't stay stuck.

CHAPTER 3
HELPFUL MINDSETS

Before we dive into the Align Your Design framework, I'd like to answer some questions I often hear from people just getting started.

How can I possibly know my purpose for the rest of my life?

The goal of the framework isn't to lock you into one specific "destiny" that defines the rest of your life. That would be unwise because your life purpose should always be evolving as you mature. So if it helps, only think in terms of your next three to five years and what you know about yourself and the world at this point in time. You can (and should) revisit these questions in the future to keep up with life's changes.

Isn't focusing so much energy on myself selfish?

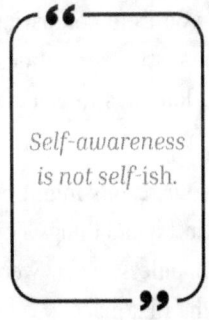

Self-awareness is not self-ish.

Yes, you're going to spend time in these exercises thinking about yourself, but when you complete the framework, you'll actually be freed up to think of yourself *less* often. After you gain clarity, you won't constantly second-guess yourself, and your thoughts won't be swirling around unanswered questions. Instead, you'll be able to focus your energies outward with confidence.

Should I focus on my work life or personal life?

You should definitely consider *ALL* aspects of your life as you progress through the framework. You are one person with one life. The demands of your job can shape your skills, but they don't change your core personality. We'll talk more about how your insights can help you maximize your work situation in Chapter 12.

What if I don't like what I find?

If you find that you disagree with an assessment or with what other people are telling you, just sit with it for a while. You could be in a blind spot, and it might take a while to see the light. Sometimes, insecurity, pride, or wrong expectations can keep us from accurately seeing ourselves. Accepting reality isn't always easy and it can be a humbling experience. But that's where true growth happens.

You may have an unrealistic view of your abilities and potential. That could be in the form of either overestimating or underestimating yourself. Your goal should be to find an accurate understanding of what you can contribute. If you thought you were going to single-handedly conquer the world, I'd rather burst your bubble now and have you focus on engaging the practical things right in front of you than to waste years chasing a fantasy.

This is where true humility comes in. Even though the word is not popular, humility is a good thing. Humility frees you from comparing yourself to others and burdening yourself with unrealistic expectations. And it unchains you from chronically unfulfilled longings to achieve things you aren't really designed to accomplish.

> *You can't be disillusioned unless you were believing an illusion in the first place.*

So, in a way, some of your results might be disillusioning, but that isn't a bad thing. You can't be disillusioned unless you were believing an illusion in the first place.

Let's go!

OK, that's enough background.

No more delays and no more excuses.

Let's get started.

PART 2
THE ALIGN YOUR DESIGN FRAMEWORK

CHAPTER 4
ASK YOUR PEOPLE

OTHERS CAN SEE YOU BETTER THAN YOU SEE YOURSELF

It's amazing how you can have exceptional talent and not recognize it until someone else sees it in you. That's the story of Viola Davis. She grew up in poverty, and her path to acting success wasn't easy. Even as she began to win recognition, she struggled with self-doubt and deep-seated insecurities. When she was cast to star in *Doubt* with the legendary Meryl Streep, Viola was nervous and intimidated. How could she possibly be good enough to work with an actress who had been, at that point, nominated for fourteen Academy Awards and won two of them?

After they had performed a particularly intense scene together, Meryl Streep turned to Viola and told her, "You're my favorite actor."

What an astounding moment! One of the greatest actresses of all time just told her she admired her work. Streep's words let her know that her skills and talent were evident to the people around her.

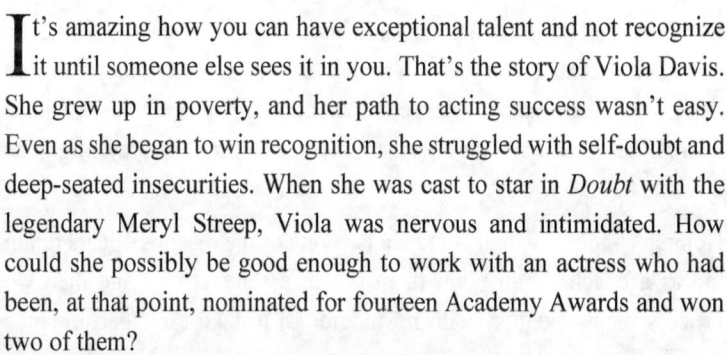
> *Other people can often see you more accurately than you see yourself.*

Viola didn't overcome her insecurities all at once, but hearing how she was seen by someone she respected helped her to emerge into her own remarkable acting success.

The Principle

What Meryl Streep did for Viola Davis is a good example of our first important principle: Other people can often see you more accurately than you see yourself.

Why is that? Well, you've lived with yourself your whole life, and you've gotten used to yourself. That makes it hard for you to see yourself objectively and causes a phenomenon called a blind spot.

You may know about blind spots from driving a car. There are some things you can't see when you're in the driver's seat looking in the side view mirrors. Other vehicles are actually there, but they're hidden from your view.

Blind spots in our lives act the same way. They can lead you to excuse bad habits because you just don't see them anymore. But they can also cause you to discount your exceptional talents. You're so close to those talents that you don't see them anymore even though they might be obvious to others.

Helping to identify their blind spots is one of the reasons clients retain me as a coach. I can point them out in a safe setting, and then we process them together (with no judgment) to take their performance even higher.

This process of getting feedback from others is like a 360 review you may have experienced in your workplace. In a 360 review, you try to get a full range of perspectives—from superiors, peers, and subordinates—on how you're doing. It gives you a better picture of yourself because it brings you feedback from people who see you from different perspectives.

See It In Action

One of my executive coaching clients, Mack, gained very helpful insight as he applied this principle. He sent a short survey to five former coworkers, asking them each to identify five positive qualities they see in him and one or two negatives.

The responses mentioned different traits that were very affirming, but one consistent theme that stood out was his loyalty and positive belief in people. Those traits come so naturally to Mack that he never thought they were exceptional and didn't fully realize the effect that his leadership had on his employees and the teams that he built. This insight helped him gain confidence in his specific leadership style and the impact he wanted to make in the world.

Interestingly, this same quality was also mentioned as a negative when it was overplayed. Because Mack has such a positive view of people, he is slow to accept that some people are just toxic and don't deserve his full trust. When conflicts arose, his first instinct was to internalize the problem and think, "Maybe it's me."

All of this was good information, but its value really came to light two years later when he was promoted to a new organization. It wasn't long before an insecure leader felt threatened by his leadership and tried some manipulative tactics. During that conflict, Mack remembered the feedback he received two years prior and was able to tell himself, "Maybe it's *not* me; it's probably *them*!" He literally took a screenshot of the survey feedback and posted it where he could see it and really let it sink in.

Navigating through that conflict gave him newfound confidence, eliminated self-doubt, and was a significant point of growth in his leadership.

Apply It

How can you get beyond your blind spots to truly see your own strengths and weaknesses objectively? Let's start with some reflection questions.

Recall: For What Do People Compliment You?

The first question is: for which skills or personality traits do people tend to compliment you? Write down all the repeated compliments you hear, whether you believe them or not. You could be discounting these affirmations because they land in a blind spot. Even if you don't think the compliments are sincere, it doesn't matter. Write them all down.

Recall: When Do People Say You're Too Hard on Yourself?

For your second reflection question, think of a time when you might have been hard on yourself when performing a task or skill. You might have internally criticized yourself, but someone else commented something like, "Hey, why are you being so hard on yourself? You're really good at this." If you've heard words to that effect, write down the talent or skill that you were using at the time. And if you can, list two or three of those instances.

Seek Feedback: Five Strengths and a Weakness

People don't always share their opinions with you, so for this next part, you're going to actively solicit their feedback. Think of people who've seen you in action on a day-to-day basis. These could include current and former co-workers (including superiors, peers, and subordinates), family, extended family, friends, neighbors, and so forth.

I want you to email or text at least five people and ask them to name the top five strengths they see in you and one weakness. You want them to be as candid as possible. Keep these tips in mind when you ask people for their feedback:

1. Don't ask toxic people, people who constantly criticize you, or those who are always negative. That could do you more harm than good.
2. Don't ask people who only tell you the easy, nice stuff. You want people who are going to be honest with you.
3. When you ask, be specific about when you need them to reply. "Could you please get back to me by next Friday?" If they don't, send them one reminder. You're not nagging them; they just may have forgotten.

4. Obtain at least five completed responses. If you can get ten or more, that's ideal. Not everyone might respond, so the more people you ask, the better. One of my clients actually asked forty-five people! He got great results from his efforts.

Now, collect their feedback and look for patterns. What qualities showed up more than once? If you see similarities, even if people used different words, circle them because these clearly indicate one of your strengths.

It's also important to realize that when other people describe something as a possible weakness, it is often a strength that's just being overplayed. Too much of a good thing can annoy or alienate people. For instance, someone's feedback might say, "You talk too much." Well, it could be that you have a strong communication talent that needs to be regulated a bit.

Another example could be that you like to be helpful by solving problems and fixing things. But taken too far, it can come across as intrusive ("too helpful"), and you may be denying others the opportunity to solve their own problems. So, I want you to take any weaknesses people report and see if they correspond to a strength you have. You just might need to tone it down a bit.

After you've completed the reflection questions and analyzed others' feedback, select the top three to five insights that you got from this chapter. Then, record those under the heading Ask Others in whatever you're using to take notes.

In the next chapter, you'll discover how science can give you additional insights into your unique design and amp up your self-awareness.

Ask Your People: Summary

The Principle: Other people can see you more clearly than you see yourself.

- You're too close to yourself, so you have blind spots.

- You may be blind to your exceptional qualities.

- The compliments you receive are a clue—even if you don't fully believe them.

- You may need to solicit this kind of feedback from the people in your life.

Take Action!

- For what do people compliment you?

- Where might you be too hard on yourself?

- Solicit feedback from at least five people.

My MVP (Most Valuable Point) from this chapter:

CHAPTER 5
ASK AN ASSESSMENT
TOOLS REVEAL HOW YOU'RE WIRED

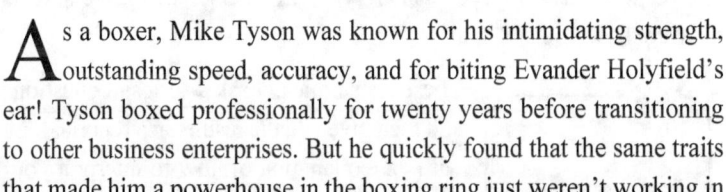

As a boxer, Mike Tyson was known for his intimidating strength, outstanding speed, accuracy, and for biting Evander Holyfield's ear! Tyson boxed professionally for twenty years before transitioning to other business enterprises. But he quickly found that the same traits that made him a powerhouse in the boxing ring just weren't working in business.

Tyson credited the DiSC® personality assessment tool with helping him understand his specific communication and leadership style. It taught him how to adjust his dominant (high "D") personality to better fit in the business world, where nuance is rewarded.

After he made the adjustments, other people started to notice that he was presenting himself as a more friendly, less confrontational person. This led to new opportunities, including acting, speaking, exhibition boxing, and creating the Legends Only League for retired professional athletes.

The first Legends Only bout, a pandemic-period pairing of Tyson v. Roy Jones, Jr., generated $80 million in pay-per-view revenues.

The Principle

The study of human development and personality theory has advanced exponentially in recent years, and I want you to be able to take full advantage of what's available.

Maybe you've heard the saying, "Everyone is a genius. But if you judge a fish by its ability to climb a tree, it will live its whole life believing that it is stupid."

I don't want that to happen to you. Instead, I want you to know who you are and how you are uniquely wired so you can focus your life on accomplishing the things that suit your design.

An IQ test measures how smart you are. Personality assessments measure how you are smart.

> "
> *An IQ test measures how smart you are. Personality assessments measure how you are smart*
> "

These tests typically ask a series of questions and then give you the results in a report, along with an explanation of how to interpret your scores. Different assessment methodologies measure different aspects of your design, so it's best to take at least two different assessments. This will help you get a fuller perspective of your unique talents, your personality leanings, and the way you tend to view the world.

See It in Action

Youssef was ambitious, smart, and got good results. But he came from a Middle Eastern culture that rewarded debate and a confrontational communication style. Now living in the US, he would need to make some adjustments in order to succeed.

Because of his drive, he advanced quickly through the corporate ranks in his twenties and thirties. But, in his early forties he found himself being passed over for promotions and receiving negative comments during his performance reviews. He took the Gallup CliftonStrengths® assessment and together we discovered that his strengths were focused on a powerful combination of Strategic, Analytical, and Command talents. And he scored very low on Empathy and Harmony.

As his leadership coach, I worked with him to identify and systematically review these talents as well as the potential blind spots that can come with each one.

- His Strategic thinking caused him to be impatient with people who couldn't see the way forward as quickly and clearly as he could.
- Other people would feel "interrogated" by him when his Analytical talent would ask for more details and challenge assumptions.
- And his strong Command talent conveyed a directness and candor that intimidated people.

With this new self-awareness, Youssef was able to work on how he came across to others and develop better emotional intelligence. He made huge improvements, and at his next evaluation, these were some of the comments from his co-workers:

- "I want to be on his team."
- "He's a natural leader."
- "He cares about how I feel."

He also developed better relations with his wife and kids, and he soon landed a new, more influential role at a different company.

Apply It

Your exercise for this chapter is simply to take two assessments. They measure different things, which is why I want you to take two. If you've taken one or more of these before but it's been several years since, you may want to retake it. I list five popular ones here, but there are many others. Most of these are free or have free versions available.

27

- **Gallup Clifton Strengths®** is one of my personal favorites. It used to be called StrengthsFinder, which ranks thirty-four areas where you may have natural talent. Unlike the other assessments listed below, it does not try to put you into a category. Instead, your combination of strengths paints a picture that is uniquely you. This assessment is particularly helpful for knowing what you can contribute to your work environment and what kinds of roles might suit you best.

  To access this test, go to: https://store.gallup.com/p/en-us/10003/cliftonstrengths-34

  There is no free version.

- The **Enneagram** has seen a surge in popularity recently. The Enneagram identifies nine dominant personality types, which are reflected in the ways we process life's inputs. It will measure your motivations and the way you tend to view the world.

  Learn more: https://www.enneagraminstitute.com/how-the-enneagram-system-works

  Free test: https://enneagramtest.net/

- **The Myers-Briggs Type Indicator® (MBTI®)** uses yet another approach to explain and measure aspects of personality. The sixteen personality types were created in the 1940s, with the aim of helping people discover their own strengths and gain a better understanding of how other people are different.

  Free Test: https://www.16personalities.com/

- **DiSC®** measures your behavior in terms of assertiveness and whether you are task or people-oriented. It's especially helpful as you interrelate with others, whether as peers or in work groups. It's used by more than 1 million people every year to improve work productivity, teamwork and communication.

Free test: https://www.123test.com/disc-personality-test/

Paid: https://www.discprofile.com/what-is-disc/overview/

- **Motivational Gifts**, like these other tools, is a statistically validated gifts assessment. It will help you describe the way you see the needs around you and how you naturally try to make a difference in the world.

  Free test: https://www.gifttest.org/

These assessments can be helpful, but too much information can also be overwhelming. I don't suggest you try to take all of them at once, so take just two at most for now. And you may want to take a different one not listed. By all means do so.

After taking those assessments, simply go through them and list five to ten characteristics that you agree best describe you. Also, list up to five insights you may have gained through the process. Record these under the heading "Ask an Assessment" in whatever you're using to take notes.

In the next chapter, we'll examine how some of your biggest setbacks in life can potentially point the way to your purpose.

Ask An Assessment: Summary

The Principle: Assessment tools can give you new perspectives on your personality, motivations, work styles, and communication approaches.

- These insights will give you understanding and language to explain how you're "wired."

- These insights can also help you make choices about the types of work to pursue and what to avoid.

Take Action!

- Complete two assessments.

- Identify at least five qualities about yourself that showed up strongly in the assessments.

My MVP (Most Valuable Point) from this chapter:

CHAPTER 6
ASK YOUR SETBACKS

YOUR TESTS BECOME YOUR TESTIMONY

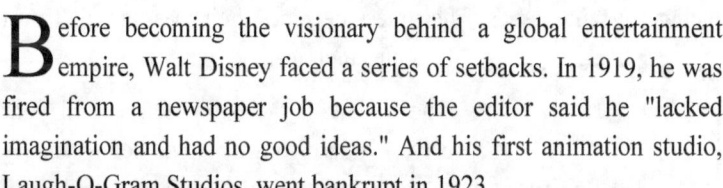

B efore becoming the visionary behind a global entertainment empire, Walt Disney faced a series of setbacks. In 1919, he was fired from a newspaper job because the editor said he "lacked imagination and had no good ideas." And his first animation studio, Laugh-O-Gram Studios, went bankrupt in 1923.

Despite these early failures, Disney didn't give up. He moved to Hollywood, eventually creating Mickey Mouse in 1928, a character that launched his career and laid the foundation for his legendary company.

Over many years of innovation, his career seesawed between financial successes and losses, but he kept identifying new creative projects that drew audiences and investors. Some include the Disneyland and Disney World theme parks, television broadcasts such as *The Mickey Mouse Club*, and popular music recordings. He received twenty-two Academy Awards for his studio's films, which is still a record.

The Principle

We learn more from our mistakes than we do from our successes.

Life can be hard—*really* hard. And it's often not fair. You may have suffered through some big failures, tragedy, injustice, abuse, neglect, relational pain, physical pain—the list goes on. But the key isn't whether or not you have pain. We all do. It's *how you handle* the pain that matters.

These challenges helped shape who you are, and if you've worked through them, you've learned some valuable lessons. And now you have experience that can be a help to others facing similar situations.

A person to whom things come easily may not be able to explain their technique. But a person who faced an especially difficult challenge had to learn things the hard way, step by step, until they found success. They are in a much better position to encourage and instruct people facing the same issues. Their mess becomes their message; their test becomes their testimony.

> *Your mess becomes your message. Your test becomes your testimony*

One caveat: if the pain itself is still your driver, you've got work to do before you try to help others. It's ironic, but to live in reaction to an event or injustice is to continue to be defined by it. It's producing a different outcome, but it's still the motivation for your actions, so you're not truly free from it. We sometimes see this dynamic in people who grew up basic necessities. They may work extra hard to become wealthy and successful to have financial security, but at their core, they may still feel like they never have enough.

This exercise asks you to identify pain and setbacks that you've reconciled inside yourself so that you have empathetic tools to help others. You may not feel you've entirely overcome some of your challenges, but that doesn't mean you're disqualified. You're still in a better place to help others if you've made some progress along the journey.

See It In Action

I'm going to tell you part of my own story that shows how I was able to find a new direction because of a hurdle that occurred over and over in my professional life.

I've spent much of my working life with technical types. I have an engineering degree and worked for twenty-two years in software start-up companies. My work life has been focused on launching new technology products, starting new companies, opening new departments, and running strategic planning functions.

As I did this, and especially as I worked with strategic partners at other companies, I was exposed to many leadership and management styles. It got to the point where I could sometimes accurately assess a company culture within minutes of speaking with an employee. I could discern things like:

- This CEO doesn't delegate authority and has become a bottleneck in the organization.
- This founder is in love with his own technology and doesn't pay attention to what the market actually wants.
- This company does (or doesn't) understand the need to emphasize benefits to the user more than the technical features of the product.

I could see where wrong strategic decisions caused business problems and where a leader's lack of self-awareness became the limiting factor for the company's success. But I also found that it's very hard to affect change with leaders and founders as an inside employee. It was especially vexing when I could see what was wrong but was not empowered to make the changes. This led to a lot of frustration and wasted years at one company. It wasn't getting results, and my input wasn't welcome.

I could have gotten cynical and bitter, but one way I got through these frustrations was to mentally log each lesson I learned so I could leverage them sometime in the future. Fast forward to 2016, when I became an executive coach/consultant. Now, I can draw from those hard lessons to quickly and tactfully help my clients see their blind spots and improve their leadership skills. I also leverage those years of painful learning on a consulting basis for strategic planning, team building, and helping companies pivot into more profitable business models.

Apply It

1. What was one difficult challenge you've had to overcome in your personal or professional life?
2. Explain how you overcame (or made progress toward overcoming) the challenge you named in question 1.
3. How did this challenge change you as a person? What lessons/ life principles/ wisdom did you learn?
4. What can you now offer others due to having worked through this?
5. Can your lessons be summarized in a concise message or philosophy? If so, what would that be?

Feel free to perform this same exercise again using different challenges you've faced.

Record the answers to the five questions under the heading Ask Your Setbacks in whatever you're using to take notes.

In the next chapter we'll explore the deep passions of your heart. They aren't always obvious, but I have some tools that can help bring clarity to what's truly important to you.

Ask Your Setbacks: Summary

The Principle: Overcoming difficulties qualifies you to help others dealing with similar issues.

- Life is hard. Everyone experiences pain.
- The question is: What will you do with your pain?
- People who have overcome pain are the best teachers.
- People who are still holding onto pain can get stuck.
- Pain can give us more compassion for others.

Take Action!

- Complete the reflection questions in this chapter.

My MVP (Most Valuable Point) from this chapter:

CHAPTER 7
ASK YOUR HEART

YOUR PASSIONS FUEL YOUR ACTIONS

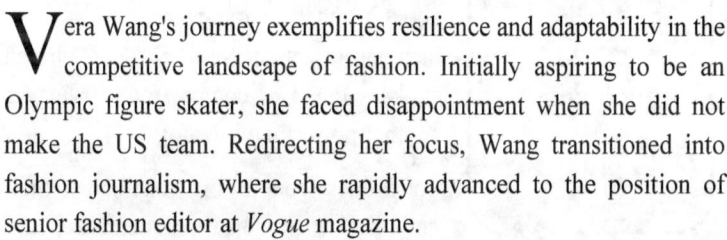

Vera Wang's journey exemplifies resilience and adaptability in the competitive landscape of fashion. Initially aspiring to be an Olympic figure skater, she faced disappointment when she did not make the US team. Redirecting her focus, Wang transitioned into fashion journalism, where she rapidly advanced to the position of senior fashion editor at *Vogue* magazine.

During her tenure, Wang immersed herself in the industry, and a desire to create her own designs began to grow. At age forty, she took a significant career risk by leaving *Vogue* to design accessories for Ralph Lauren. That change further clarified her vision and helped develop her creative aspirations.

Wang ultimately opened her own boutique specializing in bridal wear, which quickly expanded to include bespoke cocktail dresses and ready-to-wear collections. She strategically diversified her brand to encompass fragrances, home products, and jewelry, positioning herself as a prominent figure in the fashion industry.

By embracing change and following her passion for design, Vera Wang not only achieved significant business success but also redefined her professional identity, making a lasting impact on the fashion world.

The Principle

We usually think of passion as a strong emotion, but the word is used so often nowadays that it has become trite. What you're passionate about is not what thrills you, what you enjoy, or what is fun. To be passionate is to love something so much you're willing to sacrifice for it.

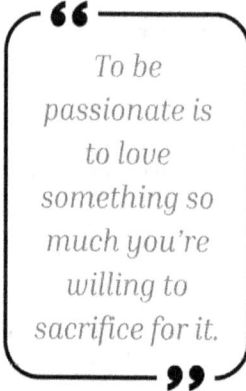

To be passionate is to love something so much you're willing to sacrifice for it.

Passion can manifest in a wide range of emotions, including anger, excitement, and compassion. You wouldn't feel angry about something unless you cared deeply about it, and that passionate anger can drive meaningful action. Similarly, passion can evoke sadness or compassion, serving as another powerful motivator.

Sometimes, people lose touch with their passion when the practicalities and pressures of everyday life cloud their focus. Paul, a client of mine, launched multiple entrepreneurial ventures as a young man, and he had aspirations of building his own company. But as a married man with a young child, he knew he needed a steady income to support his family.

While lamenting that he had no time to start a side hustle, he received a pivotal insight through a journaling exercise I designed (I'll explain that process in more detail in Chapter 9). He realized his best career option was to establish himself as an entrepreneurial practitioner *within his current company*—an "intrapreneur"—instead of trying to start his own business. He didn't need to abandon his dream of becoming an entrepreneur. Instead, he could channel that passion into a different setting and still find fulfillment. Incidentally, he's now thriving in his corporate role.

Desire vs. the Object of Desire

Your passion is the deep desire that drives you, but not necessarily the specific *object* of your desire. For example, you might want to own a house (the *object* of desire), but the underlying passion could actually be to provide secure housing for your family. The object of your desire is often the thing you think will fulfill your passion. But what if there are other ways to get that fulfillment?

Knowing the difference between your deeper desire and the object of your desire is essential. But if you haven't listened to your heart, you might think they are one and the same. And this can lead to unnecessary regret.

My friend Bob studied physical education in college with the aspiration of becoming a sports coach. An injury sidelined that dream, and decades later, he wound up as the administrative pastor of a large suburban church. He wasn't the person preaching from the pulpit. Instead, he oversaw the background administrative functions, providing leadership and guidance to the many people who kept the ministries and facilities running well.

One day, as his long-standing regret of a lost coaching career was getting the best of him, he talked to God about it. And then his big epiphany occurred. He actually WAS a coach, but just not on the sports field. He was coaching a team of "players," bringing out their best talents, and leading them toward a unified goal.

That "Aha!" moment gave him a new perspective on his life and helped him re-engage his career with newfound vigor and purpose.

See It in Action

Sometimes, people just need to be validated for their passion, especially if it's visionary. The first time I met with Roy, I wondered if there was any enthusiasm left in the man. He was unhappy and unchallenged at his job. He was commuting more than an hour each way every day. And, as is often the case, the overall drain left little energy for a focused job search in his free time.

Here's a key principle to remember: Burnout doesn't happen from working too hard. It happens when your work is misaligned with your design.

> **"**
> *Burnout doesn't happen from working too hard. It happens when your work is misaligned with your design.*
> **"**

In Roy's case, he's a thought leader and strategic networker, but he was stuck in a role that required routine maintenance and very little decision-making.

As a trained coach, I kept asking him targeted questions to uncover his deeper desires. Eventually, he mentioned that he wanted to become a Chief Information Officer, and he had a strong vision to reinvent that role. He believed the modern CIO should own the company's strategic planning process in order to enable the business goals with the right technology. But he had dismissed the idea as too far-fetched given his current situation.

Have you ever noticed in a conversation when someone's face lights up? When their eyes get wider? When their tone of voice and body language shift? Those are clues that someone is speaking from their passion. That's what I saw in Roy when he described his vision. I knew we had tapped into his heart's desire. "That's exactly what you need to pursue," I told him.

Roy left our meeting a different man. *Within three weeks,* he found a new job much closer to home. One that challenged him, paid better, and allowed him to realize his vision of redefining his CIO role as a CeXO (Chief Execution Officer).

Apply It

These questions are designed to surface the passions and interests in your heart. There is no right or wrong response length to the questions here. Use them as prompts to generate your thoughts and write as much or as little to express what's in your heart. Try answering at least seven of the ten questions.

1. What about life really energizes you and stirs your passion?
2. What is a problem or issue in the world that really gets you really angry?
3. What is a problem in the world that makes you sad to the point of tears?
4. Did you ever make a costly personal sacrifice to right a wrong or to build something meaningful? What was that cause or issue?
5. At age 12, what did you want to be when you grew up? Was there a person or event that inspired you in that direction? How about at age 18?
6. What's one thing that, even if you could get paid for it, would you do for free because you love it so much?
7. What's one topic that, when someone asks you about it, you can't stop talking?
8. When do you find yourself in your "zone"—enjoying yourself, deeply immersed in activity, and completely losing track of time?
9. What are some favorite quotes, sayings, or religious verses that inspire you?
10. Who are some of your heroes or role models (either real or fictitious)? What qualities about those figures inspire you?
11. Is there a certain people group, age bracket, subculture, or population that you are naturally drawn to? If so, who are they, and how would you like to help them?

Now go back and review your answers to these questions. Look to see if there are any themes or commonalities across your answers. Are there things you never noticed before? Record those insights under the heading "Ask Your Heart" in whatever you're using to take notes.

The clues to your life purpose are often scattered like breadcrumbs in the trail of your history. In the next chapter, I'll introduce you to a powerful tool that identifies when your best self has shown itself in your past.

Ask Your Heart: Summary

The Principle: Your passions can ignite action.

- A passion is something you love so much you're willing to sacrifice for it.
- Passion can be marked by deep joy, but it can also show up as anger.
- There's often a difference between your desire and the object of your desire.
- When you know your passions, you can direct your life to leverage them.

Take Action!

- Complete the reflection questions in this chapter.

My MVP (Most Valuable Point) from this chapter:

CHAPTER 8
ASK YOUR HISTORY

YOUR PAST HOLDS POWERFUL KEYS TO YOUR FUTURE

You may know Rick Steves, the travel writer and television host. But did you know that his first trip to Europe was completely against his will? At the age of fourteen, his parents and grandparents reluctantly dragged him along to visit Norwegian relatives.

Yet, during that first visit, he began to discover how distant cultures have both differences and similarities. For example, he compared the taste of the Norwegian orange soda, Solo, alongside his beloved Fanta. And he also came to realize that the family bonds transcend geographical borders.

After college, Rick fed his growing passion for travel, working various jobs across Europe, eventually establishing a life pattern of spending a third of every year overseas. Back in the US, he taught adult education classes on travel sharing slideshows and insights he gained from his experiences, and he opened a travel center where he organized tours. He also self-published his first guidebook, launching a successful career that would eventually include numerous books, television shows, and apps.

Rick's journey illustrates how past experiences can shape your future. By learning from his trip to Norway, he not only carved out a successful career for himself but also inspired countless others to travel for themselves.

The Principle

In this section, you are going to take a look back into your history and mine patterns that identify the skills and talents that you enjoy using.

You were born with certain innate talents, but you've also developed certain capabilities that have become a part of who you are. When you use those skills and talents, it brings you enjoyment which usually leads to good results as well. Some people call that "being in your zone." It's where you tend to do your best work, and it just so happens to be where you can make the most impact in the world.

> **"**
>
> *No matter where you go, there you are.*
>
> **"**

By looking at instances from your past where you experienced success, you can find patterns that most likely predict how you'll thrive in the future. As the saying goes, No matter where you go, there you are.

In a sense, you're going to look across history to see past versions of "you" in multiple settings.

See It In Action

Jim had amassed some very impressive accomplishments in his career. He headed the worldwide IT operations group for a global pharmaceutical company and had built data centers for some huge retail brands. But when I met him years later, he was stuck in a lower position doing boring work, a victim of workplace ageism.

He engaged me as a coach through a mutual friend, and we used the Align Your Design framework to help him transition his career. As he worked through the Ask Your History exercise, he wrote out seven stories about times when he felt successful in the past.

Several patterns emerged across his stories. But Jim's biggest "Aha!" moment was when he recognized that in many of his past successes, other people relied on him to run critical operations. And he really enjoyed that level of responsibility and the challenges that came with it.

This new insight changed his outlook, and we decided to highlight that characteristic to redefine his professional brand. His new LinkedIn profile statement read, "Both the CEO and COO of a global pharmaceutical company said they sleep better at night knowing I'm at the controls."

Wow! That says a lot, doesn't it?

What I don't want you to miss is that *Jim was actually using these strong qualities all along*, but because he didn't have the clarity to articulate them, he couldn't present his exceptional value to his employers. And they, in turn, didn't give him the respect and authority that he rightly deserved. When he got the clarity he needed, it wasn't long before he found new work that was meaningful and challenging. He felt like he was thriving once again.

Apply It

This process is about looking at times in your past when you felt a sense of accomplishment or success. Then you'll reverse-engineer those moments to identify what you do best and what comes naturally to you.

When I did this exercise myself, I recognized that many of my past successes had come when I initiated new projects and events. I had never previously noticed that pattern, and that one insight helped to shape many of the choices I made in my career path from then on.

Some Notes Before You Begin

You'll probably put more time into this exercise than any of the others, but it typically yields the most valuable insights. And the results you get are highly leverageable in job interviews if you're seeking to make a career change. Therefore, I encourage you to give this your best effort. Don't skip it, and don't cut corners.

The following technique is based on and expanded from exercises in Richard N. Bolles's book, *What Color Is Your Parachute*, a resource I highly recommend to my career coaching clients. For additional insight, you could get a copy of that book and reference "Petal 3" of the flower diagram—what he calls your Transferable Skills.

Step 1

Start by identifying an event in your life when you felt a sense of accomplishment and satisfaction. Write this story out using the following format:

1. What did you want to accomplish?
2. What challenges got in the way?
3. Describe what you did step by step to accomplish the goal, specifically identifying the skills and talents that you used.
4. Describe the result. And if that result can be measured, note the specifics.
5. Give your story a title.

Tips:

- Each story doesn't need to be long. Four paragraphs are plenty.
- Don't spend too much time on the background of the story. Focus your writing efforts on the skills and talents that you used.
- Focus on the *skills* that you used, not the *personality traits* that also supported your success. For example, you might write, "I organized a large team into smaller groups and gave them

specific assignments," versus "People responded to my enthusiasm." Organizing and delegating are *skills*, but enthusiasm is a *personality trait*.

- YOU are the audience for the story, so you don't need to go into long explanations, and it's not going to be criticized or evaluated by anyone else.

- You don't need to look for huge, blockbuster events from your past. Normal scenarios are fine. You're looking for the good feeling *you* had of success or accomplishment.

- Stories that happen across shorter time frames are better because it's easier to identify the specific skills involved. Consider writing about a specific project that you worked on instead of longer goals, such as obtaining a college degree.

- Think of stories from different time periods in your life, even when you were a child or doing school projects. Variety is a good thing. And the stories don't have to be all work-related.

- You certainly don't have to do this in one sitting. Write out one of the stories, take a break, and write another story at another time.

Step 2

Now, go back through your story and circle all the words that identify a skill or talent that you used. Then, write each of those skills in a numbered list on a separate page of your notes. Use one line for each skill.

Step 3

Now, write out six more stories, repeating steps 1 and 2. Write the story, identify the skills, and enter those skills on the list.

As you list the skills in Step 2, if a skill is already on the list, don't write it out again. Instead, put a checkmark next to where it's already listed. That lets you keep track of how many times any particular skill shows up in your different stories.

49

Step 4

Now, examine your list and look for patterns. If you see a certain skill appearing in many of your stories, that's a *huge* clue! Next, make a new list and rank-order your skills by how many checkmarks they have. The skill with the most checkmarks goes at the top of the list. The one with the second most checks is next, and so on. Only list the top ten skills.

Step 5

Finally, look to see if there are other patterns in those stories. Were there physical settings that made a difference? Are you more successful in certain reporting structures, authority scenarios, or reward systems? Do you do better with certain kinds of people? Working alone? It may be helpful for somebody else to read the stories with you to get an additional perspective.

If you recognize that your skills tend to be used in certain situations or contexts, add those insights to the skill description. For example, "good listener" may appear as a skill. But the added insight might be "good listener to people in emotional crisis who have a hard time trusting others."

Here's Where the Fun Starts

Now look at the top ten skills that appear on your ranked list.

Were you surprised by the results?

Are any of these talents or skills that you may have discounted?

Which of these skills land in the sweet spot where what you enjoy doing is also something you're good at and that other people value?

Record your top ten skills and any other insights you gained from this exercise under the heading "Ask Your History" in whatever you're using to take notes.

Ask Your History: Summary

The Principle: Your Past Holds Keys to Your Future.

- When you have been most satisfied and productive in the past, you were living as your true self.
- Your history can remind you of what you were doing at those times.
- Your history can point out what those times have in common.
- With that information, you can make smart choices about your future.

Take Action!

- Complete the story-writing and skills-extraction exercise. Write seven stories and identify your top ten skills.

Next, I'll introduce a bonus chapter that addresses the question, "Why am I alive?"

My MVP (Most Valuable Point) from this chapter:

CHAPTER 9
ASK YOUR CREATOR

YOU WERE DESIGNED FOR A PURPOSE

———————— ≋ ————————

Before we continue, I want to address the elephant in this chapter. Faith, religion, and spirituality can evoke strong feelings and disagreements, and the purpose of this chapter is NOT to challenge that. I hold a Christian worldview, but even if that's not your practice, many of the principles in this chapter will still apply. I invite you to explore these with an open mind and consider whether they resonate with your own belief systems.

In this chapter, I'm going to use the word "God" for expediency, but it is not my intention to be exclusive. If it helps you think in terms of your Higher Power, the Divine, the Universe, spirituality, or any specific name or term in your spiritual framework, please do so.

If your worldview holds that there is no spiritual dimension in the universe, you might choose to skip this chapter. The insights you gather from the other chapters will still be valuable. But you also might want to give these exercises a try. What do you have to lose?

A Visit with Mother Teresa

Several decades ago, Frank Butler, then president of Eastman Gelatine (a subsidiary of Eastman Kodak), and his wife Ruth embarked on a pre-retirement trip to Calcutta. They were exploring ways to make a meaningful impact with their time and resources and believed that volunteering with Mother Teresa's Missionaries of Charity could provide a fulfilling direction for their post-career lives. However, Mother Teresa had a different perspective.

As Frank told the story, the Butlers were seated with Mother Teresa when she reached across, put her hand on his knee, and advised them: "Go back to America. In all my travels around the world, I have never seen such loneliness as there is in the poverty of affluence." This insight prompted the Butlers to reassess their plan and reconsider how they could truly make a difference.

Upon returning to the U.S., Frank redirected his retirement efforts toward initiatives that promote social change. He became involved with Business Leaders for Sensible Priorities and Responsible Life, as well as what is now the Faith and Money Network, an organization aimed at helping wealthy individuals shift their focus from financial anxiety to a lifestyle centered on generosity, justice, and sustainability.

The Principle

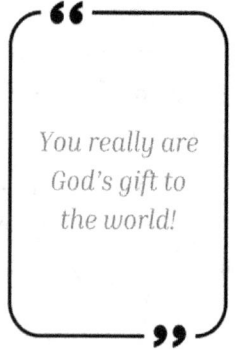

You really are God's gift to the world!

When we were kids growing up, if we wanted to cut someone down to size, we'd say, "You think you're God's gift to the world!" implying that they thought too highly of themselves. Well, the truth is, you really are God's gift to the world! The reason you have your gifts and talents is so you can use them to help make the world a better place for others—to serve humankind. God thought you were a good idea, which is why you were placed in your setting at this point in history with a certain set of talents.

It just so happens that our wonderful design as humans inclines us to find resonance, satisfaction, and joy when we operate in those very talents God gave us. This function naturally pulls us toward doing our best work. Conversely, we experience frustration and stress when we're not in alignment with our talents. That's also sending a signal to us to make corrections. It's the same dynamic in play but expressed in two different ways.

One of the Jewish prophets, Jeremiah, lays out a powerful invitation (God is speaking here): "I knew you before I formed you in your mother's womb. Before you were born, I set you apart and appointed you" (Jer 1:5 NLT). It means that before your conception, there was an intentional, eternal design for your life. And there's a purpose for your journey on earth—an appointment.

[Note: I encourage you to watch the Disney/Pixar movie *Soul*. It's one of the best visualizations of this principle that I've come across.]

So, how do you go about discovering God's design for you? Again, Jeremiah speaks: "This is God's message, that God who made the earth, made it livable and lasting, known everywhere as God: 'Call to me and I will answer you. I'll tell you marvelous and wondrous things that you could never figure out on your own" (Jer 33:2–3 MSG). In other words, God wants to tell us things beyond our human logic, but first, we need to ask (also called prayer).

At the same time, looking for answers from God will draw you into a place of mystery where answers may come, but not always when or how you expected them or as specific as you'd like them to be. Why is that? I believe there are at least a few reasons: 1) God knows what we can handle at this point in time, and out of love, doesn't tell us more than that. 2) When we follow God one step at a time, we develop the habit of listening to God and asking for guidance. 3) As we learn, by experience, to trust God's wise guidance, we learn humility and faith.

See It in Action

Jim and Isaac are two clients whose "Ask God" efforts took them in directions they did not expect.

Jim was a mid-career entrepreneur who owned a five-person design and advertising company. That business, his growing young family, and the non-profit he founded had maxed out his time but not his aspirations. He imagined doing even more but couldn't fathom how to add one more thing to his hectic life.

Jim used the process of spiritual journaling (written prayers) to get clarity. At first, most of what he wrote were honest laments. He complained to God about how he was leaving his dreams behind just to maintain his daily responsibilities and how those limitations were crowding his future vision out of view. A steady flow of emotions and thoughts came out of his pen, and after a while, he found that he was able to discern God's guidance more clearly.

Jim's big "Aha!" came when he sensed God impressing on him that his limitations in life were actually a gift. Even though they can be frustrating, they helped to ground him in his present reality and keep him humble—a needed check on his pride and self-reliance.

This helped him clarify that he was, in fact, still on the right path and helped him clarify what he could realistically take on at this stage of his life. He went from a state of being maxed out and wanting more to living well in the life he has right now. His situation hadn't changed, but he made a big shift in his attitude, resulting in peace and contentment.

Another client, Isaac, is a busy executive running a large IT division of a global bank but needed clarity on some big decisions that were coming up. He has a full house with his wife, their two young children, and his mother-in-law. If he was going to find clarity, he knew he would need to get away to a quiet space. So, he structured a one-day planning retreat, booked a hotel room, and brought a decade's worth of his old journaling notebooks with him.

First, he took a nap and watched some TV. He needed that rest. Then, as he reviewed his history and prayed about his next steps, he got a revelation that surprised him. He'd been seeking clarity from the entirely wrong perspective. He didn't need to think about "what" direction he should take. Instead, he needed to focus on the "who." Who was he as a husband, a father, a vice president, and a child of God? Who was he becoming? What character traits did he need to build in order to navigate the future challenges in his life? And who was he surrounding himself with for accountability and inspiration?

He recognized a pattern: Focusing on the "what" had caused him to overcommit, and he needed to say "No" more often so he could be more present with his existing commitments. He walked away from his retreat energized and with a fresh perspective on taking on new challenges.

The "seeking" cycle

Regardless of their faith persuasion, I notice a common pattern as people incorporate a spiritual dimension into their lives. It goes something like this:

- "I wonder about the reason for my existence. Where do I fit in the big, cosmic plan? That is, what is my life's purpose?"
- I ask God for answers.
- I get insights as to what those answers might be.
- I execute decisions in my current stage of life guided by these insights.
- As I mature, I become dissatisfied with the level of understanding I've been operating under—I want more specifics as to my purpose.
- I ask God more questions that probe for deeper understanding.
- I get deeper insights.
- I apply those.
- I mature in that stage, and the cycle repeats itself.

Apply It

Some of the "clues" God gives include the insights we've uncovered in prior chapters. Your unique design and talents are a "divine nudge" in the direction you should pursue. But you can also ask God directly. And I'd like to suggest three approaches to that:

- Reading holy texts/scriptures
- Spiritual prayer journaling
- Consulting wise spiritual directors

Reading Sacred Texts/Scriptures

The Bible, Torah, Quran, and other holy texts offer valuable guidance and wisdom, yet reading them is often neglected despite their easy availability. Occasionally during your reading, a passage may resonate deeply, "jumping off the page" and speaking directly to your heart. At other times, the key will lie in simply making scripture reading a consistent habit. Ultimately, dedicating time to spiritual reading and reflection significantly enhances your ability to discern God's purpose for your life.

Spiritual Journaling

Allow me to introduce a practice known as spiritual journaling. This is the written form of what can be referred to as "listening prayer."

First, get in the right mental state. This process can't be rushed, so set aside at least twenty minutes. Turn off your phone, TV, and any other distractions. Take something to write with and go to a place where you're alone. You might like to put on some relaxing instrumental music with no words, or you might prefer silence.

When you're ready, write down your first question for God. I've listed several below that you could use to get started. Wait just twenty or thirty seconds, then write down any impressions you've received in response to that question. Don't try to assess the accuracy of your impressions; just write them down. You will look back at them later, but that's a whole different process. Your impressions come to you through intuition and imagination, but assessment is done analytically and critically. If you try to use intuition and analysis at the same time, you'll stall the flow because they're very different cognitive processes.

Remember, no one is grading this exercise. There's no right or wrong. What you understand today might change in the future. That's okay. Go with what you have at this point. Remember that verse from Jeremiah I cited earlier: "Call to me and I will answer you." Expect that you're going to receive something.

Sample questions:

1. Dear God, what do you like best about me?
2. What purpose did you design me to fulfill?
3. What are some things that get in the way of my purpose?
4. How can I relate with you better?

You can also write out your own journaling questions and see what God has to say. Just go with the flow.

After you've recorded your impressions, then go back and analyze them. Does what you wrote sound like something you would normally say to yourself, or does it seem to be coming from another view? Does it square with sound theology? Does it come from a loving perspective? If so, then ponder these things. Maybe go back for more Q&A prayer time through your journal. If you're not sure, it's often helpful to have a spiritually mature person review what you wrote to offer their discernment and guidance.

One Note of Caution

Listening to prayer and journaling can be subjective and need to be considered in association with other factors in your life. For that reason, I do not recommend making even a moderately important decision solely on the impressions you receive from journaling. There are multiple ways of discerning God's will, and this is just one of them to consider. If God wants to steer you in a certain direction, use some other forms of discernment to confirm your impressions.

For more guidance on spiritual journaling from a Christian perspective, check out Communion with God Ministries at www.cwgministries.org

Wise Spiritual Directors

Spiritually mature men and women can be a great resource to help you discern God's purpose for your life. A priest, pastor, rabbi, minister, imam, spiritual director, or faith-based counselor has typically received training in helping people navigate existential questions. Look for someone who has a good reputation for helping others.

One key to watch for—their general approach should be to help you discern and come to conclusions for yourself using spiritual principles. That is different from giving specific advice. They should not be telling you what to do or putting themselves in the position of God.

Additional Thoughts

Here are some other ways to consider how God might be trying to communicate with you (not an exhaustive list):

1. Do you have recurring dreams when you sleep? What are the themes or messages in those dreams?
2. Have you had any "Aha!" moments in life when you felt as though God was sending you a message? List them.
3. Have you received any divine revelations or encouragement that resonated with you that were given through other people?
4. Were there times when circumstances just seemed to line up in a way to steer you in a certain direction?

Try two or three of these methods to engage God. Then, summarize the insights that you received. Record those under the heading Ask Your Creator in whatever you're using to take notes.

Would you like to accelerate your process of gaining clarity? In the next chapter, I'll show you a simple and powerful way to do exactly that.

Ask Your Creator: Summary

The Principle: You can gain useful impressions from your spiritual life.

- God designed you for a purpose.
- You're happiest and most effective when you work to your unique design.
- God wants to answer your questions about your design and purpose.
- As you listen, stay in the flow, and then sort and assess later.
- There are multiple ways to discern God's will, and you should use a combination of them

Take Action!

- Try two or three of these methods in this chapter to ask God about your purpose

My MVP (Most Valuable Point) from this chapter:

CHAPTER 10
ASK A PROFESSIONAL

A TRAINED GUIDE CAN ACCELERATE THE PROCESS

In the early stages of her career, Oprah Winfrey worked as a television news anchor and reporter but struggled in these roles. Her emotional involvement with the news stories often conflicted with the expected journalistic objectivity. She was even demoted at one point due to this.

Oprah eventually sought career guidance. She discovered that her true strength was connecting with people on a more personal, emotional level and was encouraged to refocus on her strengths and authentic self.

She shifted to talk shows, where her empathy and communication skills worked together to bring remarkable success. Oprah went on to build a media empire, becoming one of the most influential and successful talk show hosts in television history. Asking a professional for direction transformed her career.

The Principle

A professional life coach is trained to listen for the keys that will help you get unstuck and keep you moving forward. They provide objective feedback and ask powerful questions to help increase your awareness.

You may be able to eventually get some of the same results on your own over time, but a coach can greatly accelerate the process. Often, amazingly so. One of my clients was stuck in a holding pattern for decades, but as a result of coaching, has made incredible progress. He recently commented to me, "It's almost scary how fast everything is changing. If you had asked me two years ago, I never would have thought I could come this far this quickly."

Coaches help you work through your blind spots and blockages and then help you design an action plan to move forward. If needed, they can also provide accountability in reaching your goals. I have some clients who know what they need to do but meet with me regularly simply to maintain the right mindset and keep them on track. Truth be told, I hired a coach for that very same reason.

> *The biggest obstacle to transformation is, "I already knew that."*

Enlisting the help of a coach will require a certain level of humility. When deciding whether to take on a new client, I look for three "Hs." Is this person **Hungry** to grow and do the work required, **Humble** enough to truly listen, and willing to be **Honest** about their situation? As my friend Cal Chinen says, "The biggest obstacle to transformation is, "I already knew that." I've found that to be very true.

Coaching is different from therapy. Therapy typically looks backward into your past to help heal problem areas in your life. Coaching starts today, and looks forward to helping you access a better future. Both approaches can be effective, but you need to set your expectations appropriately.

See It In Action

All of the client stories in this book illustrate the power of coaching. Here's one more.

By her mid-forties, Mindy had become THE global subject matter expert in her field. She freely gave her time to help other practitioners succeed and even founded a nonprofit organization to train and credential others in her field. She traveled the world as a speaker and consultant … but she was frustrated. She found herself handholding too many junior-level professionals when what she really loved to do was pioneer change and be a forerunner and influencer in her field.

Then Mindy engaged me as a coach. We started to identify what she truly wanted in life as I made some direct observations and asked her some powerful questions. We recognized that one of her core values was freedom, but she wasn't currently living with much autonomy. She carried too many obligations and found it hard to say "no" to requests for help.

We designed an action plan that she could execute in stages. She resigned from the nonprofit because it was sapping her time and energy. She became more selective in her speaking engagements and only agreed to take the ones that would make a significant impact. She wrote a book, and she started her own invitation-only executive coaching cohort. That allowed her to spend time with the best in her field and impart her wisdom to people who could impact others. She's now living her true calling as a global thought leader with exponential influence.

Apply It

Set up an appointment with a coach. Most professional coaches offer a free "discovery call" where you can tell them what you're looking for and can ask them questions to see if the two of you would work well together.

A few things to watch for:

1. Coaching works best when you know what you want from the engagement. You may need help clarifying some specific goals, but that can be an objective of the sessions.
2. In general, coaching falls into two categories. Ask any potential coach which approach they use.

3. **Performance** coaching is where the coach passes along their personal expertise in an area (health, business, sports, etc.) and guides you with specific instructions that tell you how to improve.

4. **Non-directive** (or transformational) coaching is where the coach helps you grow in self-awareness and clarity to make your own decisions. They may offer expert advice, but only if asked. The assumption is that you have the wherewithal to direct your own life. The Align Your Design framework is based on this non-directive approach.

5. Look for some credentialing. The gold standard for non-directive coaching is the International Coaching Federation (ICF), and their helpful website (coachingfederation.org) can give you more guidance on selecting the right coach for you. I carry the Professional Certified Coach (PCC) credential from the ICF, along with several certifications through other organizations (see petecoaching.com).

6. Ask for references or case studies so you can see how others have benefitted.

7. Pricing for coaching services varies greatly, so ask the coach what their rate is and how many sessions they recommend. Many times a coach will offer an introductory package of several sessions.

Your mindset should be that this is an investment in yourself and your future. In general, I've found that you get what you pay for.

You've done a great job so far. In the next chapter, I'll show you how to collate all your insights to gain the clarity you're looking for.

Ask a Professional: Summary

The Principle: A professional coach can help you accelerate your progress.

A professional can:

- Help you gain awareness and offer fresh perspectives that you may be missing
- Tactfully help you work through your blind spots
- Help you design an action plan for your success
- Provide accountability in reaching your goals

Take Action!

- Set up a discovery call with a professional coach.

My MVP (Most Valuable Point) from this chapter:

CHAPTER 11
BRINGING IT ALL TOGETHER

Congratulations! You've gotten this far in the Align Your Design framework. This is where we bring all your work and insights together.

Some Thoughts on Finding Clarity

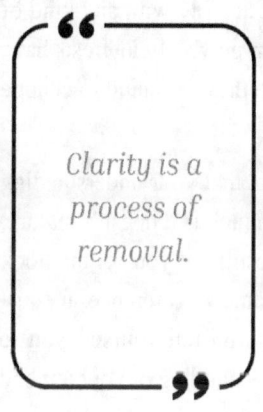

Clarity is a process of removal.

Getting clarity regarding your life purpose isn't about explaining everything in your life. Instead, it's identifying the one thing that's most important—that thing that's already inside of you—and not getting distracted by everything else. It's actually a process of removal. It's like when the sun burns off the morning fog so you can clearly see what was hiding behind the mist. Clarity takes away complications, so you see the most important thing that remains.

Misconceptions About Finding Clarity

Three common misconceptions often get in the way of people finding clarity in their professional lives.

Looking for a Silver Bullet. You might wrongly think that gaining clarity about your life purpose will answer your many unresolved issues. It won't. To be sure, clarity does help to make sense of your life and brings focus and energy, but we're talking about an overarching concept here. Clarity doesn't address every nuanced detail of your talents, history, and desires. In fact, the simpler it is, the more powerful its effect.

The antidote? Lower your expectations for detailed answers. Look for the one thing you really want to do that uses your favorite talents and propels you to make a real difference in the world. Everything else is window dressing.

Keeping your options open. Are you hedging your bets? Do you love to have a backup plan in case things don't work out? True clarity requires you to be decisive, to pick a path, and to say "no" to other options. In fact, that's a big part of its power—it clears away the clutter.

Thinking that it's carved in stone. "How can I say with any kind of certainty what I'll be doing twenty years from now? My interests have already changed multiple times in my life, so they're bound to change again."

The best way to deal with this is to just accept that your understanding of your life purpose *will* change over time. In fact, if it doesn't mature, you're not growing as a person. But that doesn't get you off the hook of needing a guiding compass *now*. As a frame of reference, try just thinking about the next three to five years. And tell yourself you're doing the best you can with your current understanding of yourself and the world at this point. You can (and should) revisit things in the future and make modifications.

Summarizing Your Work

Now it's time to gather your insights into a summary format. Think of it as your own personal mission statement. I'm suggesting three possible methods to do this. Try them and see which works best for you, then record your work under the heading Bringing It All Together in whatever you're using to take notes.

Method 1: Fill-in-the-Blanks

Look across your answers from all the chapters and try to identify any patterns, similarities, or common themes. This might be a good time to ask a trusted friend to also look at your answers to see if they see some things you may have missed.

Then, try to complete these statements by referencing the insights you received from the indicated chapters.

- **I love to use** _____ ...

  (List your favorite skills and talents here, drawing insights from the Ask Your **People**, Ask an **Assessment**, and Ask Your **History** chapters.)

- ... **to primarily serve** _____ ...

  (Identify the industry, population, or subculture you have an affinity for, drawing on insights from the Ask Your **History**, Ask Your **Setbacks**, and Ask Your **Heart** chapters.)

- ... **to address** _____ ...

  (Identify a specific need or issue you want to impact, drawing on insights from the Ask Your **History**, Ask Your **Setbacks**, and Ask Your **Heart** chapters.)

- ... **with the goal of** _____.

  (Here, describe the result you're working toward based on insights from the Ask Your **Setbacks**, Ask Your **Heart**, and Ask Your **Creator** chapters.)

Then, put it together in a single sentence. A sample result might look like this:

"I love to use my creativity, leadership, and mentoring abilities to build teams that create apps for underserved populations in order to help them improve their finances and health so they and their families can flourish."

Method 2: The Reduction Approach

This approach asks you to use the common themes and other insights you discovered from all the exercises in Part 2 and create a 100-word description of your life purpose. Write it any way you want, but start with the words "I am a person who..."

My 100-word statement:

Now, take that 100-word description and reduce it down to fifty words. Rather than trying to describe everything about yourself, just capture the most essential parts.

My 50-word statement:

To *really* capture the essence, reduce those fifty words down to just twenty words or fewer.

My 20-word (or shorter) statement:

Here are some examples of the 20-word statement:

- "I serve humanity by bringing to market breakthrough healthcare innovations that help millions."
- "My mission is to enliven, encourage, and reinspire the love of music for children in public schools."
- "I have a unique ability to win others over. My passions include family, friends, and helping those less fortunate."

Method 3: Freeform

If neither of the first two methods works for you, then go with a "freeform" method—meaning, do whatever you want! Be creative. Some ideas include:

- Write out your purpose in the form of a poem.
- Make a bulleted outline list of the important points.
- Create a picture collage with notations.
- Record a video of "Present You" talking to "Future You."

Whatever speaks to you is fair game. Just make sure it has enough referenceable points so that when you revisit it in the future you'll understand what it's communicating.

And Finally...

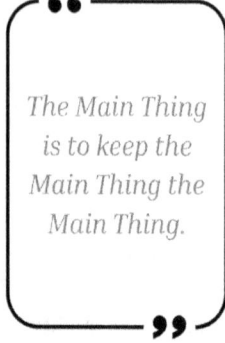

The Main Thing is to keep the Main Thing the Main Thing.

When you've captured all your hard work into a meaningful summary, put today's date on it and store it in a safe place for future reference. If you do quarterly or annual planning, it's a good idea to retrieve your summary and review it to remind yourself of your purpose. Referencing it can also serve to keep complications at bay.

The Main Thing is to keep the Main Thing the Main Thing.

Now that you've gotten clarity, how can you leverage it in everyday life? That's what Part 3 is about. Onward!

PART 3
WHAT'S NEXT?

CHAPTER 12
ALIGNING YOUR WORK

The insights you gathered from the Align Your Design framework can act as a compass in all areas of your life, including family, community involvement, recreation, etc. But the one area where most of my coaching clients want better alignment is in their work life.

When I get pushback from doubters that this process is unrealistic, it usually sounds something like this:

"This is just a pipe dream. I mean, you don't know my work situation. I can't change the requirements of my job to only do the things that I enjoy."

I have two responses to that.

1) Of course not. You still must perform in a role in order to get paid. But if you can get *more* alignment between what you do and how you're designed, it's worth pursuing. If you could get an eighty percent alignment, you'd be doing great.

2) You don't know that things can't change. The limitations you perceive might be true but they're often not the whole picture. You typically have far more options than you think you do. Sometimes, even within your existing organization.

I especially see this with people who are early in their careers. They are often afraid to ask their boss to modify their assigned role for fear of looking bad or disgruntled. What they don't realize is that oftentimes the boss *wants* suggestions to better optimize the team. And once the employee gathers the courage to make the suggestion, new doors can open up to them.

This was Ricky's situation. He came to me for coaching to get out of his current non-profit organization ASAP. As we worked through the Align Your Design framework, we discovered that he was very talented in strategic business development, and in the past had pioneered a program that performed very well but he was currently being micromanaged in a routine role that discouraged him from taking any initiative.

Once Ricky got a clear picture of what he really wanted and could describe the value that he brings to an organization (backed up with real life examples), he was all set to look for a new job. Incidentally, he was talking with a peer in another department at his current job. When he heard what Ricky was looking for, he quickly persuaded his boss to create a new role for Ricky in their business development department.

Earlier, Ricky thought he needed to quit his job. Instead, the doors of opportunity flew open for him once he got clarity. I've seen this same scenario play out many times with my other clients.

The pivot key

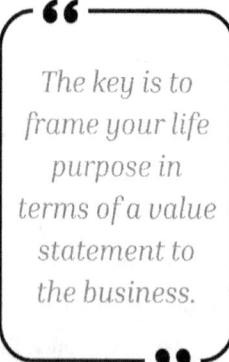

The key is to frame your life purpose in terms of a value statement to the business.

This type of pivoting doesn't just happen on its own. The key to activating it is to frame your life purpose and talents in terms of the value you can bring to the organization.

One practical way to do this is to take your results from Chapter 11 and translate them into words that show business value. Use words like *teams, profitability, employee retention, efficiency, analytics, strategy,* etc. Whatever is important to the mission of the organization.

For example, instead of "I like to start new things, experiment until they work, and then tell everyone about it," you might say, "I'm great at researching and pioneering new product offerings, finding the right messaging to penetrate the market, then handing my findings off to the sales and marketing teams to increase top-line revenue. I'm a launch specialist."

Or consider this statement: "I love math and can predict trends by getting information off the Internet. I'm also very frugal and hate to waste money. The more money we save, the more we can invest and give to good causes." It could be rephrased as "I am exceptional at researching and analyzing market trends—I'm a natural with numbers. I use those skills to optimize processes and cut costs to increase efficiency and the bottom line. I also like to champion our company's community involvement."

Of course, your statements need to be true, and you have to have stories that prove your claims. But if you did the Ask Your History exercise, you'll have some great material to work with.

If you need help translating your skills and life purpose in organizational terms, you might want to enlist the help of a career coach.

Jason Found Clarity

When we left Jason in Chapter 1, he had been unsuccessfully trying to become a chief information officer. He felt overlooked in a career that seemed to have stagnated.

After he found me as a coach, I took him through the Align Your Design framework. As a result, Jason was able to clarify what really mattered to him. His passion was to build high-performing teams that could develop products to help people take better control over their finances. He also clarified his distinctive "team coach" leadership style.

He'd been aiming for the C-suite because he thought that was the "right" path forward. But he didn't have an appetite for C-suite politics and preferred hands-on work to high-level meetings.

His "Aha!" moment came when he recognized a different way forward. He could target a role as chief product officer. The title would not be as high-paying or prestigious as CIO, but it perfectly aligned with his skills, talents, and overall life mission. Plus, it would capitalize on the part of his job he likes the best—discovering new technologies and building useful products.

In less than a week, he shed his CIO aspirations. He had been trying to expand his range of capabilities to become CIO. Instead, he did the reverse and *narrowed* his focus to becoming a specialist in product management. By our next coaching session, we had mapped out practical steps for his new career path, and his wife commented that he seemed to have a new lease on life.

In addition to serving his company well, Jason also decided to start positioning himself as a subject matter expert in his industry, seeking out speaking opportunities, writing and sharing articles on LinkedIn, and offering himself as a mentor. His new momentum was noticed by the CEO and other senior leaders at his company.

Jason got clarity about his true desires, and that made it possible for him to achieve the transformation he wanted.

Renee Found Clarity

When we last saw Renee in Chapter 1, she was overworked, overwhelmed, and underappreciated. When she engaged me as a coach and started using the Align Your Design framework, we quickly uncovered her superpower—spotting talent and knowing just the right people to bring into conversations to get results. We saw the first hint of that superpower when we "asked her history."

She remembered that back in high school, she had always hosted the cool parties everyone wanted to be at, and she realized that in a way, she was still doing that. The only difference was that now her "parties" were corporate meetings, and she still knew how to invite the right people.

> **"**
>
> *She kept waiting for her company to "pick her," but they were stalling. She was going to have to pick herself.*
>
> **"**

The one person she hadn't been inviting to the party was her own true self. She kept waiting for her company to "pick her," but they were stalling. She was going to have to pick herself.

The most important work we did together was to help her adopt a new mindset. She took control of her future using the mentality that she worked for herself. Now, she sees her employer as her main/only "client." That made it much easier for her to set healthy boundaries. And if her bosses choose not to honor those boundaries, she feels free to find another employer/client. Or she could choose to tolerate their disrespect, but now she sees that it's always her choice. It felt amazingly liberating to realize that they didn't "own" her or her future.

She found her voice and began to act out of a sense of empowerment. She talked with her boss's boss about a different role that she really wanted. To her surprise, there was no pushback at all, and she was out from under her toxic boss's influence.

We're still working on her ability to say "no," but she's come a long way. And now she has become more selective in the work she takes on and the new projects she initiates.

Jason and Renee's stories serve as examples of what's possible when you get some help and shift perspectives. What kind of transformations are waiting for you? There's only one way to find out, and that's to take action.

CHAPTER 13
TAKE ACTION!

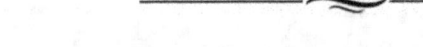

As you completed the exercises in this book, you've learned a lot about your motivations, skills, and purpose in life. But they weren't meant to be simply academic assignments. Now, it's time to put your insights to work for you.

Get to Work on What You've Discovered

I absolutely love getting a new insight, an "Aha!" moment, an epiphany. But those moments can be deceptive. If your new revelation seems profound, you may be tempted to believe that it will change your life. It certainly *can* change your life, but that won't happen automatically. It's up to you to put the work in and apply it to truly make an impact.

And these "Aha!" moments are ephemeral. The power of an insight will disappear quickly if it's not coupled with action.

Jim Rohn coined this phrase, "The longer you wait to do something you should do now, the greater the odds that you will never actually do it." A younger me thought that this didn't apply to me, and I could remember what I learned. Younger me was wrong. It applies to all of us.

Action Brings Clarity

We're trained to believe that if we think through something, we'll get clarity, and then we can act on it. In actuality, the reverse is usually true. Taking action opens up new pathways and possibilities we never considered, and then our thinking catches up. By acting, we also learn what will and won't work in a given situation through trial and error. So, if you catch yourself overthinking a possibility, just remember "A, B, C":

Action

Brings

Clarity

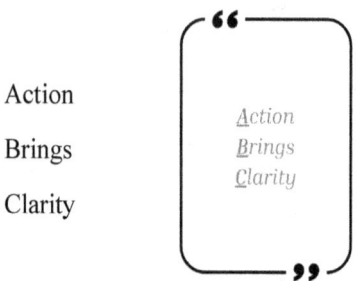

So, how do you turn an insight into an action? It's beyond the scope—or even the intent—of this book to dictate a specific action plan for you. But here's a general approach that I've found helpful.

First, identify the insight you'd like to activate. Next, ask yourself, what is the larger goal or aspiration that insight was pointing to? Then, get specific and develop a series of practical action steps that will lead toward fulfilling the larger goal.

Here's a simple example:

Insight: When I did the Ask Your People exercise, they complimented me on my communication skills. They tell me that I make things easy to understand.

Goal: I'd like to further develop my public speaking skills and get more opportunities to do training and group facilitation.

Action Plan: 1) Enroll in a public speaking course. 2) Talk to my manager about the possibility of me leading the next group training 3) Attend a Toastmasters meeting to learn about how to get speaking opportunities.

You might need help designing a plan. For instance, you may naturally find it easier to envision the big-picture conceptual goal and maybe struggle to develop the practical action plan. Or maybe it's the other way around. Either way, enlist help to fill in what you might be missing.

If the way forward doesn't seem clear to you, just take one small step even if you don't have the full plan thought out. In the example above, one small step could be to look through the course catalog at the local community college to find a public speaking class. Or do an Internet search to find a local Toastmasters meeting.

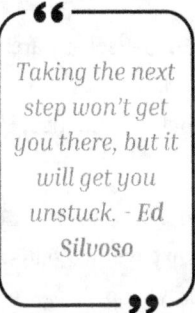

> *Taking the next step won't get you there, but it will get you unstuck. - Ed Silvoso*

As one of my mentors, Ed Silvoso, says, "Taking the next step won't get you there, but it will get you unstuck."

Set, Own, and Update Your Goals

When I look back at the times in my life when I felt the most unfulfilled, resentful, or taken advantage of, the common thread is that I abdicated my own free will. I just went along with what other people thought was best for me. This is not a good way to live your life, but it's an easy trap to fall into—and you might not realize it's happening.

Over the years I've seen one indicator that I'm starting to drift in that direction: *when I neglect setting clear goals.* A close cousin to that is when I don't update my goals based on changing circumstances. I now practice a rhythm of annual, quarterly, and weekly planning. The discipline of reviewing my goals helps me prioritize the important things and say "no" to activities that seem good but won't help me get where I want to be.

It's easy to delude yourself that you're being productive by simply staying busy. But that's not the same as being intentional and directing your life. Setting clear goals and mapping out a plan to achieve them is what turns your aspirations into reality.

The Most Important Key

Do you remember what I wrote back in Chapter 3, that self-awareness is not self-*ish*? And that if you do the internal work, it frees you up to be *less* self-centered? Well, now it's time to put that into practice. How will you direct your life toward serving others?

> **"**
> *Purpose is not just what we do, but what happens in others when we do what we do.*
> *- Dr. Caroline Leaf*
> **"**

I love this quote from Dr. Caroline Leaf, "Purpose is not just what we do, but what happens in others when we do what we do. Do you really want fulfillment? Then take your now-upgraded self and aim your talents to serve others. That's really what this book is all about—transforming your life so you can transform your world.

Theologian Frederick Buechner defines vocation as the place where "your deep gladness and the world's deep hunger meet." Your deep gladness is when you're functioning according to your design. That's where you find the most joy and satisfaction. The world's deep hunger includes all the problems in the world that are calling out to you to help bring justice and healing.

If that seems overwhelming, redefine "the world" as "your world." Not all of humanity on planet Earth, but in the spheres of influence that you can realistically reach.

Give it some thought. And maybe go back and ask God about it.

CHAPTER 14
HOW I ALIGNED WITH MY DESIGN

Back in my early twenties, when I just graduated college and was carving out my place in the world, I came across a proverb that struck a chord with me: "The beginning of wisdom is this: Get wisdom." Proverbs 4:7 NIV. That's when I realized that if I wanted to be wise, I would need to get intentional about acquiring wisdom in whatever form it came to me. From then on, I've made it my ongoing quest to collect information, amass inspiring quotes, and look for helpful tools that can impact lives.

And I started with my own life. As I've explored four different career paths, I've been collecting wisdom about who I am and how I like to work. I learn by doing, and I kept refining my understanding as I experienced more and more of life.

I like to do a lot of different things, and my careers show that. I've worked as an engineer and as a nonprofit fundraiser. I've also done business development in several technical firms. Those companies were often start-ups because, as it turns out, I like launching things. I don't provide as much value when things go into maintenance mode.

My purpose in life is to jumpstart things and then hand them off to other people. I would sometimes hear people say, "You're a good starter but not a good finisher," and I would think I was deficient. Now, I can wear that phrase as a badge of honor. Because, haters, you're right. I'm *not* a good finisher because that's not my role in life. My purpose is to start things, and not many people can do that well.

I had a big "Aha!" moment in my early thirties when I finished my second career as a nonprofit fundraiser on a high note. I dug deep into the process Richard Bolles details in *What Color is Your Parachute?*[1] and discovered that I'm multi-talented. That's why it's hard for me to fit myself into just one slot. But, I also learned that being multitalented fits very well with initiating new projects.

As I moved into high tech start-ups, I got to perform many different roles. I got to create departments, programs and products from nothing, and then hand them off to other people to grow them. I became what some people call a "serial intrapreneur." I got new things started, then moved on to start something else in the same organization.

The more I developed those skills within organizations, the more I found people coming to me to be mentored. They liked that I didn't give the same advice to everyone, but helped them identify their own sense of calling, and then helped them move forward with practical action steps. This was before I even knew what coaching was. I was just being a helpful colleague.

Then, I experienced two different tipping-point incidents. The first happened at a conference when I was in my late forties. A woman I was talking with over lunch shared that she was motivated as a leader and was very able to take charge and organize things. Her husband was laid-back and considerably less task-oriented, but they were part of a faith community that expected men to be dominant leaders of their families. She felt conflicted, and I was able to help her reconcile how she could honor her husband's role while still using her own strong leadership gift. The light bulbs came on for her, and she said, "You know, you really should get paid for this."

That's when I first started to think that this could be my job, not just a side hobby.

[1] This job-hunter's guide has been regularly updated and continuously in print for more than fifty years.

So, I started taking courses in coaching and earned the first of many certifications. In the first course, the instructor pointed out that a scary big step you must take as a new coach is asking for money for your services—a hurdle any solo practitioner has to overcome. "To get started, just offer to serve people, and if they offer you money, take it," was the instructor's advice. Well, *less than twelve hours later*, I was talking in my office with a contractor whose son was struggling. I listened, suggested some ideas, and then he sat up very straight and said, "I will pay you if you say that to my son."

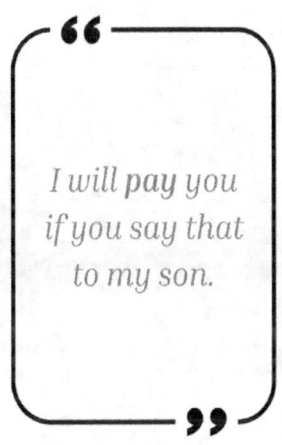

*I will **pay you** if you say that to my son.*

I could see divine guidance all over the timing of that and took it as a sign that I was ready. And so my part-time coaching practice was born.

Now, eight years later, as a full-time Professional Certified Coach, I've helped more than 300 clients transform their lives. They often come to me looking for a career change, seeking mid-life clarity, or just dissatisfied with how their lives are playing out, knowing that they have much more to offer.

Along the way, I pay attention to what gets results, and I've curated those tools and wisdom nuggets into clear, practical processes. This book reflects just one of my frameworks, which has been refined over many years and with many people.

You really can live your life with clarity and focus. It's not just a theory. I've personally lived on both sides, on the one in a state of confusion and timidity and on the other with clarity and confidence. I can tell you firsthand that clarity and confidence are much better—and they are attainable. My clients will tell you the same thing.

CONCLUSION

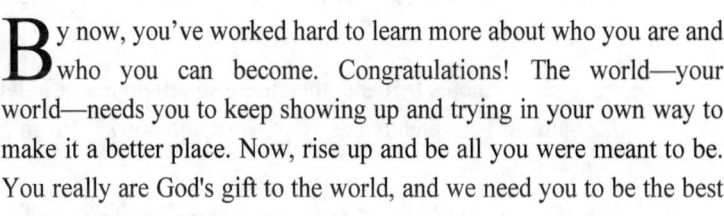

By now, you've worked hard to learn more about who you are and who you can become. Congratulations! The world—your world—needs you to keep showing up and trying in your own way to make it a better place. Now, rise up and be all you were meant to be. You really are God's gift to the world, and we need you to be the best version of yourself that you can be.

Thank you for spending time with me and letting me speak into your life. I take that privilege seriously and always strive to present a quality, actionable experience for my clients through my coaching, books, and podcast.

My hope is that you find yourself enriched and able to see yourself and others in a new way. May you feel liberated to let go of the wrong expectations and flourish according to your intended design.

An Offer

The Align Your Design framework sets a strong foundation to point you in the right direction. But you may need help formulating the next practical action steps for your goals.

If you complete the Align Your Design framework in Part 2 you can qualify for a free, 30-minute coaching session with a professional coach—a $250 USD value. These coaches have been trained and certified by the International Coach Federation and personally vetted by me.

To redeem the offer:

- You need to have completed each section of the framework. Submissions with incomplete or skipped sections won't be considered (with the exception of Chapter 9, which is recommended, but optional).

- Put your results in an electronic document file. Any standard document file will do (.doc, .docx, PDF, .txt), but it must be less than 10 MB.

  - If you took notes by hand, then use a smartphone or digital camera to take pictures of your work and copy them into one document file.

- Email your file(s) to askpete@petecoaching.com, Subject line: "Align Your Design free coaching offer." In the body of the email list your name, age, gender, current occupation, and your city, state, and country of residence. Your submission is completely confidential, and your email won't be shared with anyone except your assigned coach.

- Allow one to two weeks to pair you with a coach from our team. Your assigned coach will then reach out to you to schedule a video call and review your results with you.

Summary of the Key Principles in This Book

- You have a specific pattern—a design.

  - Your design comes from both nature (genetics) and nurture (upbringing).

- When you align your work and activities with your design:

  - You do your best work.
  - You make the best contribution to your world.
  - You're the most fulfilled.

- It's hard to clearly see your design—you are too close to yourself.
- There are multiple techniques you can use to get clarity.

- Ask Your People—Others Can See You Better Than You See Yourself.
- Ask Assessment Tools—They Reveal How You're Wired.
- Ask Your Setbacks—Your Tests become your Testimony.
- Ask Your Heart—Your Passions Fuel Your Actions.
- Ask Your History—Your Past Holds Powerful Keys to Your Future.
- Ask Your Creator—You Were Designed for a Purpose.
- Ask a Professional—A Trained Guide Can Accelerate the Process.

- Action Brings Clarity. You can't just think about these techniques, you must do the work.
- This is an ongoing journey as you grow and mature.

  - The framework should be revisited every three to five years for an update.

ABOUT COACH PETE

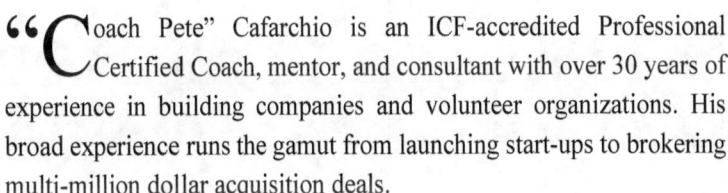

"Coach Pete" Cafarchio is an ICF-accredited Professional Certified Coach, mentor, and consultant with over 30 years of experience in building companies and volunteer organizations. His broad experience runs the gamut from launching start-ups to brokering multi-million dollar acquisition deals.

He works with leaders from all market sectors to uncover their hidden gems, develop their leadership style, and get more from their teams for exponential results. Coach Pete's clients often comment on his perceptive insights and balance between inspiring encouragement and candid, tough love.

Pete co-hosts a weekly podcast, "Transform Your Life with Steve and Pete." He's also a frequent volunteer to help the homeless in his beloved city of New York.

He holds an engineering degree from Clarkson University, has numerous certifications in coaching and personality assessments, and has developed his own online learning course— "Decoding Your Destiny."

You can contact Coach Pete and access his personal development resources at www.petecoaching.com,

TOP RECOMMENDATIONS FOR FURTHER READING

What Color is Your Parachute, by Richard Bolles
This book remains the standard for people looking to change jobs or career paths.

Mindset, by Carol Dweck, Ph.D.
Dr. Dweck's work generates more epiphanies for my clients than any other work I recommend. It presents a simple but powerful way to change the way you look at learning.

EQ 2.0, by Travis Bradberry and Jean Greaves
A simple breakdown of Emotional Intelligence concepts and practical exercises you can use to grow your EQ muscles.

The Coaching Habit: Say Less, Ask More & Change the Way You Lead Forever by Michael Bungay Stanier
The title says it all. This book is for anyone in leadership, not just professional coaches.

Strengthsfinder 2.0 by Tom Rath
Gallup has changed the name of the tool to CliftonStrengths, but this book gives an excellent summary of the 34 strengths along with practical ways to leverage each one.

ABOUT THE TRANSFORMATION STORIES YOU JUST READ

E very story of personal transformation in this book is true. Some are composites of the experiences of several clients; some are anonymized stories from one of my clients. The stories about well-known people have been compiled from a wide range of sources: print, broadcast, and online. The late Frank Butler's story about visiting Mother Teresa was first published in collaborator Carlene Hill Byron's book, *Not Quite Fine: Mental Health, Faith, and Showing Up for One Another* (Herald Press, 2021).